PROBLEMS LURK AND SOLUTIONS BREAK

FINDING A WAY FORWARD

Valsala Achuthan

Problems Lurk and Solutions Break

ISBN: 978-93-7062-326-2

Publisher

Books Mantra Publications
(An imprint of Clever Fox Publishing)
www.booksmantra.com

CONTENTS

FORWARD

Recently, I heard about a couple of people plunging into depression and a few, committing suicide. It is really disturbing to get such news. Having worked as a teacher for many years, I have a fairly good idea about the different thought patterns of children. They get upset when the elders reprimand them, when peers mock them and ignore them and they get elated when someone praises them and appreciates them. Normally, those who are good at studies are appreciated and the weak ones are either ignored or scolded. These students are not able to cope with problems.

Later, in real life too, they feel at a loss when they find themselves surrounded by different types of problems and setbacks. Isn't it the duty of all of us to make them realize the causes and consequences of these problems and show a ray of light to uplift them? This nagging thought made me write this small book. I have penned my thoughts here hoping that it will help not only the children,but also the adults.

ABOUT THE AUTHOR

Mrs. Valsala Achuthan worked as a teacher at Bhavan's Rajaji Vidyashram for 29 years. She retired as the HOD of the English department there. Now she is teaching students online. She has already published two books—Assorted Musings and A Peep into the Past. Her articles, poems, and short stories in English and Malayalam have seen print. Her pastimes are listening to music and playing chess.

CHAPTER 1

FINANCIAL PROBLEMS

"Mens sana in corpore sano" is a Latin phrase which means, "A healthy mind in a healthy body." This was written by the Roman poet, Juvenal in the first or second century AD in his SATIRE X. Even in those days people accepted the importance of having a healthy mind and its impact on our physical health. Let's analyse the problems that lead to calamities. The biggest issue is MONEY-related. Money is needed for everything and anything. From our day-to-day needs to the education of children and hospitalisation of the sick, everything demands money. When one knows that for all these things money is needed, it is the need of the hour to save as much money as possible. Some people live in ostentatious luxury. Their main aim is to flaunt their wealth and win others' admiration! On the contrary, instead of winning admiration, they imbibe jealousy. These people don't know how to spend money sensibly. Then they start borrowing money from others. They fail to handle money wisely. One borrows money from others and initially returns it but slowly abstains from returning it. He spends more and more. This would end up in pleading for more time to return the borrowed money. The lender would ask for the money back, but the borrower wouldn't, and he falls into the sludge. The borrower then would justify his stand and declare that the lender was not a good man. At length, both end up in arguments and severed relationships!

There was one family that had been living in Delhi for more than 22 years. The father of the family was well placed, and they had three children – two daughters and one son. The three of them were not very brilliant, but they graduated, and the son got a chance to go abroad. After the retirement of the man of the family, the parents and the girls returned to their native place. Unfortunately, they didn't save anything substantial. They had to live on the pension of the gentleman. They were spendthrifts and didn't have any control over the money. Fortunately, the boy got a job abroad.

That was the silver lining on the cloud . He made money and sent the father a large amount every month. Seeing the money flow, they again indulged in spending unnecessarily. The father loved boozing, and he called his friends at home. They all played cards together, then ate good food his wife made and left happily. The parents didn't feel the necessity to save money. Suddenly, letters from the boy became very few. In those days even phones were not very common, let alone cell phones. Money flow started reducing and eventually stopped.Later, they came to know that the boy married a foreigner and settled down there. The financial condition of the family became very bad.

When such problems stare at one, the solutions whisper.

First of all, there are different decent ways for making money. Those who don't have a regular job or income can think of generating money by doing some jobs like imparting knowledge of something to others. For example, you may be good at painting or drawing, sewing, cooking, singing or dancing. It is always good to spread this to others who are interested. Remember not to give any knowledge free which doesn't have any value! The service providers can collect an amount for sharing their skill. Just borrowing money from someone is not practical.

You must have heard Aesop's story of the goose which laid golden eggs. The farmer sold the eggs and with that money lived happily for some time. But then he suddenly became very greedy, and he cut open the stomach of the goose to take all the eggs together and sell those and become rich immediately, and the goose died instantaneously . The production of golden eggs stopped. That was the end of his good time.

Bearing this in mind and resolving to get out of the ditch, each member of the above family started ruminating on the various options available. No sooner did they start opening their eyes than the options unfolded. It was like a drowning man clutching a strand of straw. Catching hold of that, they pulled themselves to the shore! If one is in utter necessity and if he/she has an urge to uplift him/herself, something favourable will happen! Surprised?

But try and try.The mom was a good cook, whereas the first daughter was good at teaching. The second one was good at drawing and painting. The girls started teaching small children and painting pictures and selling. Mom prepared good food and they started supplying the same to the needy people nearby, collecting a reasonable amount. After struggling for a couple of years, they came out of their financial strain.

We must learn how to use or spend money. You should be frugal. Plan everything beforehand. Remember not to overspend. When you buy things, think about whether you really need those, and if you feel those are indispensable, go for them.

Remember, "Do not save what is left after spending, but spend what is left after saving." This was said by Warren Buffett, one of the most successful investors in the world, who was known for his simplicity in spite of his immense wealth and also his philanthropy.

Give at least 12% of your profit to do philanthropic work. Catching hold of all your money all the time won't work. You should have compassion. Keep your eyes open to help the extremely needy people. Don't bother to entertain those who unnecessarily spend money just to show off. Be selective. What you give with a sincere heart, you will get back.

CHAPTER 2

PHYSICAL HEALTH ISSUE

The second one is the health issue. "Health is wealth" is a popular saying. Some will disagree with the fact that food is the key to more robust health. Overindulgence in food items high in carbohydrates, saturated fats, and sugars are reasons for obesity, and now not only children but also adults gratify themselves by devouring different types of edibles and junk food that are available. Sedentary life, along with this, will spoil one's health. Fast food stores are ubiquitous, and their advertised, mouthwatering food items entice any foodie. A sedentary lifestyle is a concomitant contributor to the rocketing health issues.

Lack of physical health will lead to degeneration of mental health too. Alcoholism is rampant in society, and those who don't drink are considered useless. Once you start using alcohol, it becomes a habit, and for every silly reason, one starts drinking. Many say they consume alcohol to forget worries—worries at home, worries in the office, loneliness, lack of confidence, money problems, love failure, sexual problems, and health issues. As far as they are concerned, for anything and everything, alcohol is a solution. Earlier, it was the pastime of men, but now even women drink.

Initially, only society ladies used to drink. Seeing them, the others also started. Big companies encourage people to drink, and so does the government! Are these companies or organisations concerned about the well-being of the people? Not at all! They want their revenue to increase.

There was a shocking incident of a man and wife of a wealthy family drinking together and playfully tying bath towels around each other's necks.

After some time, both were fully drunk, and the husband accidentally tied the knot too tight around the wife's neck, strangling her, and she struggled and died gasping for breath!! He later surrendered to the police, and imagine the fate of the whole family!

How does one become addicted to alcohol? Initially, it starts with friends or peers persuading or coaxing or even jibing the person. Then slowly it becomes a necessity. The alcoholic becomes helpless, and he won't be able to help himself.There are times when, despite being admitted to a de-addiction centre, he is not rescued!. His internal organs will bear the brunt, and at last he will succumb to permanent sleep.

Be bold enough to admit that you have a problem before it is too late and seek help. Undoubtedly, well-wishers, immediate family members, and counselors will lend their support. Choose the friends sensibly. Indulge in any creative activity. When the mind is focussed, it becomes creative, and slowly the bottle slips and shatters.

To maintain good health, think of consuming a balanced diet every day, consisting of proteins, minerals, carbs etc. Make sure that grains, fruits, vegetables, and nuts are consumed in the right proportion. Fibre helps you free your bowel. Health experts like ayurvedic practitioners and naturopathists say that taking a teaspoon of ghee on an empty stomach is beneficial. Also, there should be six varied tastes in our food: sweet, salty, sour, hot, astringent and bitter.

Only when you are hungry do you eat. Always leave the stomach a little empty. While eating, don't drink water. Switch off the TV and mobile phone when you eat. Chew the food well and swallow. It's always good to offer silent gratitude to all who have worked behind the scenes to provide our meals. Once a month or so one can have a pizza or burger, keeping the limit in mind.

Make sure that you have enough exercise. Gyms are mushrooming everywhere, but it is not necessary to visit one. Walking is the best exercise. Just think of walking early in the morning, enjoying the beauty of nature – the rising sun, peeping through the clouds, birds flying in a particular pattern, their chirping, the blooming flowers, the aroma of coffee, mild music coming through the radio… Enjoy all these, refresh your mind, and you can feel the magic.

Like walking, jogging, swimming, cycling…all these are good. However, consider your age and see whether you can do these easily, without straining. Then indulge in these activities. Consult a doctor too.

For aged people, mild exercises like walking barefoot on the lawn, or in the house, simple eye exercises, stretching hands and legs for sometime, laughing loudly etc are recommended. Is it enough to keep your body fit? No. Your mind also should be healthy. Don't get upset by hearing criticisms. Look at the politicians. They don't give two hoots about whatever comments are passed about them. Even while addressing a large number of people, their unflinching attitude keeps them in good stead.

CHAPTER 3

MENTAL HEALTH ISSUE

Mental health and physical health are interrelated. Those with fragile minds find it difficult to confront challenges and may collapse under even minor stress. Constant nagging and scolding by the parents, arguments with the peers, abuse and molestation by the relatives and, to top it all, reprimands by the teachers and elders… all these shatter the minds of not only the children but also the affected adults.

If they have any support system or something to fall back on, they can be rescued.

In some families, children are like caged birds. They don't have a say in anything, and the elders should chalk out plans for them. What they couldn't achieve in life, the parents want the children to achieve. No one will accept the fact that their child is average at studies. Their other capabilities, the parents are not ready to accept! Moreover, nowadays parents have a tendency to teach their very young ones to remember or by heart certain facts and figures and display their ability in front of an audience or channel. They make the child get a place in Guinness world records and many other platforms. In my opinion, that is quite unnecessary for if the child is not able to maintain his popularity even when he grows up what a terribly disappointed person he would be! Guide the children, identify their potential and encourage them to tread their path without fear of falling. If he falls, give a helping hand and help them get up and try again.

The children should be taught to try again and again without getting disheartened by their defeat. Likewise, if your partner has some talent, help her/him pursue that without getting jealous of her/his achievement.

Only egocentric people will discourage a person from giving up his/her talent. However, the affected person should not get disheartened. Adults should be aware of their rights. Also, children need not have to succumb to the whims and fancies of the adults all the time.

Here, spirituality will help to a great extent. From a young age, introduce them to the power of the almighty and the scriptures of different religions, which depict stories with morals. Each one's understanding of the concept of God and the power of the Almighty differs. As the children grow, their ideas and perspectives also change. Still, their mind will somehow decipher the inner meanings, and that will help them face the challenges.

Ultimately, turning to a counsellor can provide the support the affected person needs. They should not be considered guilty, but make them realise that they are not solely responsible for the troublesome situation.

The counsellors first give them a patient hearing without being judgemental, unlike others. They help them think and analyse the problem faced by the victim and lead him/her through the right path. Now-a-days, most of the schools in India have counselors. This has a great advantage. No one outside school knows when a child has counseling. The parents refuse to take their children to a counselor because of the stigma attached to the visit. Each listener will add some colour to the fact, so if a person has a headache, by the time the news goes through ten people, the interpretation will be that the person is mad!

There was a person called Dinesh near our house. He had a mild headache initially and was taken to the doctor. He gave the man some medicine, and he became all right. But then it started repeating, and the visit to the doctor became very frequent. Once, their neighbour asked the man's father what had happened to the boy. After listening to the father, the neighbour told his wife the news. The very imaginative wife told her friend that the boy was suffering from some acute problem and both of them wondered whether there was a tumour in his head! The story went on like this and at last when he took leave for a week from office to attend a function in his native place news spread that he was hospitalized.

Imagine the condition of the man and his relatives! People started eyeing him suspiciously, and it devastated him. The rumour even spread that the boy was in a mental asylum undergoing treatment!

CHAPTER 4

VARIED PROBLEMS

Children's issues are slightly different from adults' problems. At home, children are always dominated by adults who normally feel that the little ones don't know anything and they are not capable of giving any solution to any problem. Children look for love and appreciation and acceptance. They don't appreciate any comparison. Each child is different. They are like flowers in the garden. Look at the flowers. They are of varied size, colour, fragrance, and uses. Children are also like that. Each one's interest, talent, perspective, and mood are different.

Another heartbreaking problem is they are often misguided and lured and molested. These will leave deep scars in their minds, which deepen if not addressed properly on time.

Girls have to be very careful. But boys are not spared. Once, a group of boys was playing in the big compound of a friend's house. The ball rolled out of the open gate, and the boy who went out to retrieve the ball was abducted by a stranger and taken away, but he was not able to go too far. The boy was very bold, and he screamed loudly and bit the man here and there. Since it was very painful for the abductor, he left the boy and ran to the car that was waiting there and escaped with his gang.

When the boy returned after a long wait, all shattered, his friends asked him what had happened. He narrated the whole thing, and they decided to tell their parents. That was the best thing to do. If something like this happens, let them inform their parents and also friends so that the friends also will be careful. Encourage the children to go in a group wherever they go till they are old enough to take care of themselves.

Children can sometimes come out with wonderful ideas. Give them a chance to express their view. Even if you don't accept it, they won't feel bad. On the contrary, they will feel happy that their views are considered.

you can explain to them why their view is good or why it is not acceptable. Don't ever compare a child with another one because each one's capacity and talent are different. Everyone can't become a doctor or engineer or an IAS officer. Likewise, everyone can't become an artist or a cook. We have to teach them the dignity of labour at a young age. Parents and teachers should find out the area of interest of each child and promote that.

you can explain to them why their view is good or why it is not acceptable.

They should be made aware that it is very important to take care of themselves and their safety. At a very young age they should be taught what is a good touch and what is a bad touch. If they are not comfortable with any touch, they should say, 'No,' very boldly, and they should be encouraged to discuss everything with their parents, especially Mom. Don't believe all the relatives are good, and try not to entrust the kids with relatives. Grandparents will take care of the kids, but not everybody else. Of course, there are exceptions. It is very unfortunate that there are even paedophiles! Even when other children come home to play, keep an eye. Some, without any inhibition, caress and fondle others, which may later lead to unwanted intimacies!

CHAPTER 5

ADOLESCENTS' PROBLEMS

Adolescents are not very much different from children. They too feel hurt when they are scolded or reprimanded or compared or ignored. They should not be scolded for getting poor marks or for not eating as much as the adults feel they should.Each one's talent and capability is different.

At this age they fall into bad habits. Because of peer pressure or pressure from some adults, they start smoking, drinking and even using drugs. This age is a curious age. Some may indulge in sex and even unnatural sex.

Schools have to be very careful. It is their responsibility to take care of the students as long as they are in school. It is the great responsibility of the teachers to ensure that the children are not harmed or misused by their peers and also any other miscreants in the school. It can be another teacher or a peon or anyone who enters the school discreetly.

The school administrator should be very strict, and he/she should take a group of teachers into confidence, and they should plan a strategy to be of help and solace to the children. Students should have the confidence to go to one of these teachers and open their minds to them. Let there not be too many teachers in that group because too many cooks will spoil the broth.

At home, address the adolescents as friends so that they will confide in you, the parents. Have at least one meal, preferably dinner, together. Ask them about their school or college or friends. They should feel assured that they can confide in their parents. In case they experience anything bad, let them open their hearts to their parents and siblings. They are the ones who can extend a helping hand. Sexual abuses are very common at this age. They may need counseling. Don't look at such children with suspicious eyes; instead, console them and suggest ways to avoid such experiences.

Encourage all adolescents to get involved in some sports and extracurricular activities. Let them not get glued to the TV and mobile. Let them read books that give new or interesting information. Let the peers have a discussion under the guidance of adults.

In some places, there are book clubs attached to the public libraries. There the students can get together and discuss the theme of some of the books worth reading. A few teachers also can be part of these. This habit will even urge them to continue with such discussions even after they take up jobs. This is a good pastime, unlike drinking and gossiping!

CHAPTER 6

GENERAL

Altogether, everyone has problems. The way each one handles the problem is different. For solving the problems, everyone should have the support of others. Just because one became the victim, the others should not blame or make fun of her/him.

Controlling one's mind is very important. Meditation helps in controlling the mind. There are various types of meditations. One can choose any one. At least for 15-20 minutes one should meditate. Concentrate on your breath. First, take a bath and then meditate. It's ideal to meditate in the morning. But now, people's working time is different. Many work at night. Ofcourse, students may not be able to meditate in the morning and go to school. Those who work at night also can't meditate in the morning. They have to sleep in the morning. The whole circadian rhythm is affected. One has to find a solution for this. My sincere hope is that in all the schools, the world over, meditation will be introduced.

All over the world, Yoga Day is celebrated. Yoga and meditation together can do wonders. The difference is that yoga can be practiced at a young age, but meditation is for people of a slightly more matured mind. In the topmost classes of school, it can be taught.

Let me introduce you to the different chakras of the human body. There are mainly 7 major Chakras. These are PowerPoints. Energy enters the body through these Chakras. There are various healing techniques which have to be learnt through a proper master. The master has to explain everything to the disciple and teach him/her these healings. Your honesty and integrity play a major part in making you a good healer. It's not child's play. One should understand the importance of these things, and also, you should never overdo things. It may result in your own downfall. You should not become another Dr Faustus.

Let's understand the Chakras. The lowest one is the Root Chakra, or Mooladhara. Above that is the sacral or navel chakra. Then comes the solar plexus, then the heart, followed by the throat chakra, then the third eye or agna chakra and then the crown chakra. The following picture will give you an idea about the position of various chakras. Those who haven't heard of these chakras, just have a look at the picture and try to understand their positions.

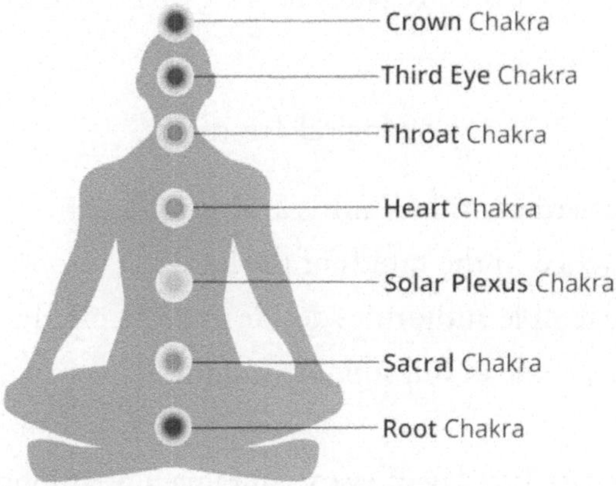

There are various healings like Pranic Healing, Reiki, Magnified Healing, etc. It is always good to learn any healing. Only adults are taught these healings. You can heal others and do self-healing too.

Try to learn more about these energy points, and you will definitely be interested to know more about these.

Meditation and the unwavering faith in the Almighty will definitely help us overcome our problems and difficulties.In fact, in villages, where there are no proper medical facilities, whenever people encounter problems, they go to the temples for solace. In my native place there is a temple where the oracle gives some solutions for the problems of families. Regarding that, I've written a poem that was published in an anthology, "Growing Pains," compiled by Mrunal Rajadhyaksha. I would like to share it with you.

"A Psychological Treatment."

The verdict of the Tantris and astrologers
Is etched in the minds of the locals.
The temple authorities decide to do an offering
The people in full support running.

The last Tuesday of every Sauramasa, year long
The Devi has to be dedicated the renowned song-
'Dharika Vadham', the proper way
With proper rituals, they say.

Invite they an oracle, to go into a trance
Listening to the rendering and move in a prance
The oracle, not fully attired, first treads
Round and round the temple, retreads

Then, increasing the pace, unties his long hair,
Speeds up to the Sanctom Sanctorum with debonair
'Hiye' is the word uttered by him.
In a trance, he enrobes with red prim,

The holy cutlass like weapon is taken,
The belled waist belt is shaken.
Like the harbinger, the oracle
Waits for the divine miracle-

The Devi entering his swaying body,
Catching the entrance of Her abode, 'Hiye' he roars
Then, facing the crowds, pours
The Devi's instructions and words

The audience, all ears, assemble like herds
Devour the decree with bemusement
The Devi speaks through this Medium
Whatever they wantto hear with tedium

The trembling stops, he catches the door at the threshold
The Devi leaves his body and enters Her idol, behold
He comes out of his trance;
The awestricken people look with confidence!

A wonderful psychological treatment this is!
The tranquil people walk away with ease!
No doctor,no medicine can compensate this!
Malls, theatres, beaches, the villagers miss,

They shed their worries
By appeasing God, listening to their stories
What a wonderful world this is!

The ordinary people of these villages don't know anything about psychology or depression or psychological treatment. Instead, this is their psychological treatment! For anything and everything, they depend on God, the supreme power.

Nowadays, people are so feeble-minded that they even think of ending their lives at the slightest provocation. All those reasons that push the people into depression may sometimes lead to their committing suicide.

Students who score poor marks, people who face humiliation from others, people who face immense challenges, those who experience love failure, and people who have extreme money problems, health issues, sexual issues—all these people are likely to at least try to end their lives. And the ways they adopt for this are the most pathetic. The most common method is by consuming pills or poison. Cyberbullying and drug addiction are the other reasons.

Some may try to cut the vein or jump from a multistoried building. A few resort to hanging themselves. Many are provoked by their own guilt!

Some force others to end their own lives. Let's understand one thing—

no one has the right to end one's own life. Even law doesn't allow that . It's a criminal offense. If anyone attempts, he can be arrested.

Think of the various options which will rescue you when you are in a problematic stage. Solutions will unfold. Think of the people who can help you out. Take help from them.

Write down the problem in a piece of paper, burn it, put the ashes in a bowl of water and flush it down. This will help you flush out the thought from your mind!

There is hope. From 2003. World Suicide Prevention day is being observed. It falls on the 10th of September. It is estimated that around 700000 people commit suicide every year world wide. If you take the total count, you will see that the suicide rates have increased too much in the recent years world over! It is found that the most vulnerable are the young adults, the ones who have to lead the world! Isn't it high time that we did something to save the world?

There were so many poets and writers who ended their lives. Virginia Woolf (1882-1941) had acute depression, which led her to drown herself in the Ouse River. Ernest Hemingway (1899-1961), the American author, was suffering from depression, paranoia, and alcoholism, and he shot himself dead.Sylvia Plath (1932-1963) was an American poet. She had bipolar disorder. She put her head into the oven to commit suicide. In this century also we hear of suicides. In fact, the number of cases has increased.

Doctors and psychiatrists believe that much can be done to prevent suicides. It's a collective responsibility. It should start with the family. Family members should look out for the symptoms like withdrawal from interacting with others, getting irritated at the slightest provocation, mood swings, too much thinking and showing disinterest in otherwise enjoyable activities.

Educational institutions also should do their bit to ensure the well being of students. The next one is the work place. Give a helping hand to each other. Let the society not criticise those who have suicidal tendencies and at last,let the media don't cook up stories about those who attempt suicide.

If you take the case of India, many celebrities commit suicide inspite of being successful!

Together, we should strive to build up a healthier society, healthier world.

Try to first listen to those who seem to be affected and then tell them the importance of their existence and suggest ways to serve others. First make sure that you really want to help. Collecting information from the affected person, and instead of helping, spreading the news about them will only worsen the situation.

There are some organizations that volunteer to help people with suicidal tendencies. If you become part of these, you can help many. Sometimes, just a phone call will help them. Those who have suicidal tendencies are given some phone numbers. They are instructed to call any of those numbers whenever they feel too disturbed. A few minutes' talk with someone will ease their minds.

There was a girl who had some problems at her husband's place. She consumed a handful of sleeping pills but thought that she would inform her sister. Knowing that something was wrong with the girl, the sister rushed to her house, took her semiconscious sister to the nearby hospital, and informed the doctors about it. Immediately, she was given the necessary treatment, and she came out of the scary situation.

First, let us understand that suicide is not the solution for anything. You consider your life valuable. Think of the positive things you can do when you are alive. Your problem is temporary. Even life is transient.

CHAPTER 7

KARMA

Everyone must have heard of the Karma theory in Hindu philosophy. According to that, whatever we sow, we shall reap. If we do good karmas, we'll get good results, but if we do bad karmas, we'll be penalised. We may see good people suffering. It is believed that they are suffering because of the bad karma of their previous birth.

There are different types of karmas – Sanchita Karma, Prarabdha Karma, Kriyamana Karma and Agami Karma.

Sanchita Karma is the accumulated or stored Karma—accumulated from your previous lives. Prarabdha Karma is the allotted Karma, that is, a subsection or a selection of your accumulated Karma. Agami Karma is the future or forthcoming karma because of your actions now. Kriyamana Karma is present actionable Karma. This has immediate consequences of your karma—good or bad.

This is to make everyone understand that whatever karma we do bears the fruit. In certain cases, the result may be immediate, and in some other cases, the result may come much later. It may come even in the next birth. Sometimes we may wonder why such a bad thing happened to someone who had done only good deeds in this life. Sanchita Karma works here. If one bears this in mind, he/she will be able to accept that. You have seen very young children suffering. That is the result of the Sanchita karma. Keep doing good deeds in this birth. That will help one reduce the impact of the previous lives' karmas.

So, let us all do good deeds, and if we encounter problems, let us take help and sort that out . Let us hope for a bright future. The wheel of time is moving. We are in the Kali Yuga now. It is moving towards Satya Yuga. So there is hope.